My First Spanish Picture Dictionary

Illustrated by Nick Sharratt

Written by Christine Mabileau and Irene Yates

Consultant Editors Natasha Farrant and Ginny Lapage

BARRON'S

First edition for the United States and Canada published by
Barron's Educational Series, Inc., in 2001.

Published by arrangement with HarperCollins*Publishers* Ltd

First published in 2001 by HarperCollins*Children's Books*,
a division of HarperCollins*Publishers* Ltd

Text and illustrations copyright © 2001 by HarperColllins*Publishers* Ltd

All inquiries should be addressed to:
Barron's Educational Series, Inc.
250 Wireless Boulevard
Hauppauge, New York 11788
http://www.barronseduc.com

International Standard Book No. 0-7641-5437-0
Library of Congress Catalog Card No. 2001087556

Printed in Singapore by Imago
9 8 7 6 5 4

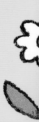

Contents

How to use this book

Tom

Elisha

Jake

Children love playing with words, and learning a new language can be lots of fun. This colorful dictionary is specially designed to help you introduce your child to Spanish. With your help, your child will learn key words from a range of familiar situations, discovering new sounds along the way. They will also start to recognize some of the differences and similarities between Spanish and English.

First steps to learning Spanish

As soon as they are comfortable expressing them- selves in their own language, children are ready to learn a new one. To get the most out of this book, sit with your child and encourage them to look at the pictures, to say the Spanish words as often as possible,

Read the heading out loud so your child knows the context of the Spanish words.

Point to the picture, then run your finger along the Spanish words, from left to right, saying the words out loud. Ask you child to repeat the words, not forgetting to say the short word in front.

Compare the Spanish word with the English, pointing out the similarities as well as the differences between the two languages.

Look for me on every page – sometimes you will have to look very hard! It's fun to see what I'm doing.

Having fun at preschool

la computadora
computer

la maestra
teacher

el libro
book

el gato

las tijeras
scissors

la acuarela
paint

el pincel
paintbrush

los gises
crayons

el pegamento
glue

12

and to answer all the questions. Come back to the book time and time again, so your child absorbs the new sounds and learns to associate the Spanish words with the pictures.

Questions and answers

Nick Sharrat's lively scenes will help your child to memorize the Spanish words by putting them into context. They also offer plenty of scope for further questions, so you can encourage your child to practice speaking their newly learned words. For your own guidance, there is a pronunciation guide at the back of the book.

Ask the questions, encouraging your child always to answer in Spanish. (The answers will be words featured on the spread.)

Encourage your child to point out and name real objects around them whenever possible.

Make up your own questions, based on what's going on in the picture. Once your child has learned about colors and numbers (see pages 40–43), you can incorporate these in your questions too, for example, "How many paintbrushes can you count?"

Learning the names of the characters will add to the fun your child gets from using this book.

Ask your child to match objects in the main picture with those shown on the left, and vice versa. When looking for an object, encourage your child always to use its Spanish name.

Lucy

Taz

Amy

Fun and games at home

la puerta
door

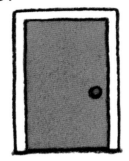

la ventana
window

la silla
chair

el sofá
sofa

el cojín
cushion

el reloj
clock

el televisor
television

el teléfono
telephone

Look at me!

la cabeza
head

el cabello
hair

la cara
face

la nariz
nose

los ojo
eyes

las orejas
ears

los dientes
teeth

la boca
mouth

el cuello
neck

el hombro
shoulder

What do you smell things with?

8

Come to my birthday party

el balón
balloon

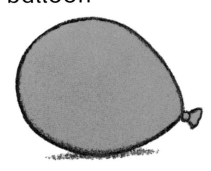

la máscara
mask

el regalo
present

el gorro de fiesta
party hat

el helado
ice cream

la torta
cake

el jugo de fruta
fruit juice

los caramelos
candy

Having fun at preschool

la computadora
computer

la maestra
teacher

el libro
book

las tijeras
scissors

la acuarela
paint

el pincel
paintbrush

el pegamento
glue

los gises
crayons

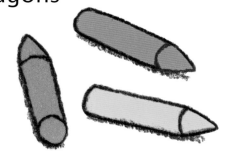

What do we like to wear?

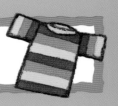

la chaqueta
jacket

la camisa
shirt

el pantalón
pants

la falda
skirt

el vestido
dress

el pantalón corto
shorts

los calcetines
socks

los zapatos
shoes

What do
you like to wear
best?

14

What do you wear on your hands?

el pijama
pajamas

la camisa de dormir
nightgown

el calzoncillo
boxers/
underpants

la braga
panties

el suéter
sweater

la camiseta
T-shirt

el gorro
hat

los guantes
gloves

Let's play in the yard

la cortadora de césped
lawnmower

la carretilla
wheelbarrow

la mariposa
butterfly

el pájaro
bird

la regadera
watering pail

la bicicleta
bike

la piscinita
kiddie pool

la flor
flower

Take a walk down our street

la casa
house

la tienda
shop

el policía
policeman

el camino
road

el automóvil
car

el farol
street light

la silla de ruedas
wheelchair

el semáforo
traffic light

Where do you go to buy things?

18

Things that go

los patines en línea
rollerblades

el camión
truck

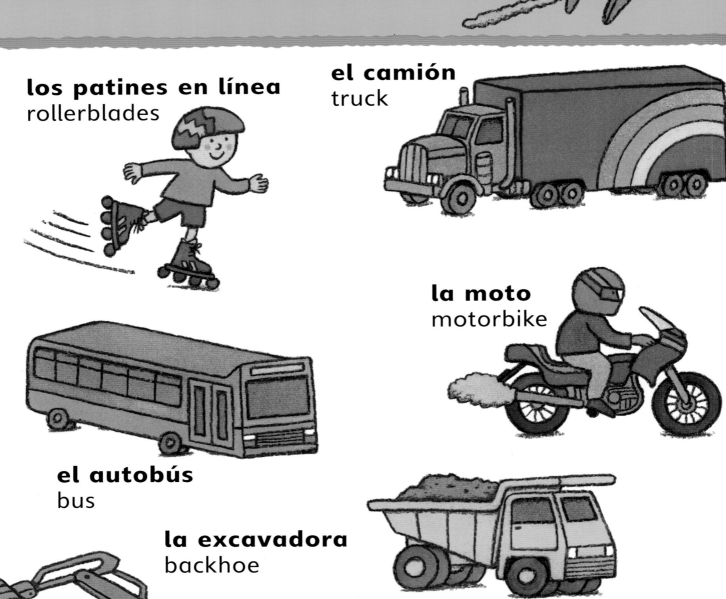

la moto
motorbike

el autobús
bus

la excavadora
backhoe

el volquete
dump truck

el barco
ship

el monopatín
skateboard

Let's go to the toy store

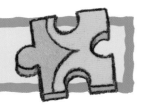

el rompecabezas
jigsaw puzzle

el camión
truck

el garaje
garage

la casa de muñecas
dollhouse

el osito de felpa
teddy bear

la muñeca
doll

la marioneta
puppet

los cubos
blocks

At the supermarket

el tarro
jar

la bolsa
bag

la lata de conservas
can

la canasta
basket

la carretilla de compras
shopping cart

el dinero
money

la caja
checkout counter

la botella
bottle

24

Food to help me grow

la fruta
fruit

las legumbres
vegetables

el arroz
rice

la hamburguesa
hamburger

las papas fritas
French fries

el espagueti
spaghetti

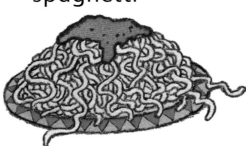

el cereal
cereal

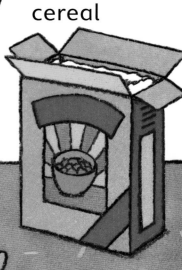

What do you eat for breakfast?

26

Take me to the pet store

el conejo
rabbit

el gatito
kitten

el pez de colores
goldfish

la jaula
cage

el hámster
hamster

el perrito
puppy

el cesto
basket

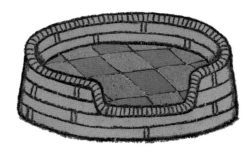

el periquito
parakeet

What's in the park?

el tobogán
slide

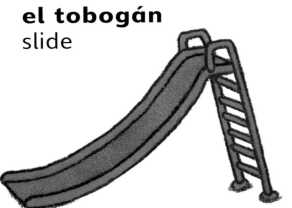

el columpio
swing

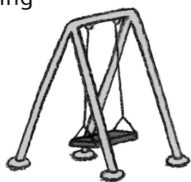

**el cochecito
de niños**
stroller

**la armazón
para trepar**
jungle
gym

el banco
bench

el árbol
tree

el perro
dog

el pato
duck

Big beasts and minibeasts

el canguro
kangaroo

la jirafa
giraffe

el león
lion

el panda
panda

el elefante
elephant

el cocodrilo
crocodile

la ballena
whale

33

Down on the farm

el granjero
farmer

el tractor
tractor

la gallina
hen

la oveja
lamb

el caballo
horse

la vaca
cow

la barrera
gate

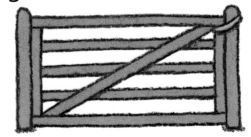

el heno
hay

A sunny day at the seashore

la concha
shell

el cangrejo
crab

la gaviota
seagull

el castillo de arena
sand castle

la pelota de playa
beach ball

la ola
wave

el balde
pail

la pala
shovel

36

See what we can do!

él salta
he jumps

él camina
he walks

ella corre
she runs

ella aplaude
she claps

ella lleva
she carries

What is the girl with the box doing?

él pinta
he paints

ellos bailan they dance

violeta
purple

rojo
red

negro
black

azul
blue

amarillo
yellow

What color is the bouncy castle?

Come and count with me

1 uno

2 dos

3 tres

4 cuatro

5 cinco

How many windows does this house have?

Count the spots on the ladybug.

6
seis

7
siete

8
ocho

9
ueve

10
diez

All year round

lunes
Monday

martes
Tuesday

miércoles
Wednesday

jueves
Thursday

viernes
Friday

sábado
Saturday

domingo
Sunday

el día
day

la noche
night

What day
of the week
is it?

What makes you put up your umbrella?

el sol
sun

la lluvia
rain

el viento
wind

la nieve
snow

How the words sound

A guide to pronunciation

Spanish pronunciation is different from English, and some Spanish sounds do not exist in English. Pronunciations are shown in italics, and stresses are shown by a " ' " sign.

Note that there is only one way to pronounce each vowel. **A** is pronounced like "ah" ("*apple*"); **E** like "eh" ("*egg*"); **I** like "ee" ("*meet*"); **O** like "oh" ("*all*"); **U** like "uh" ("*put*"). The **J** sounds like an "h," **Z** like an "s," the double-L, **LL**, is pronounced like a "y," and the **Ñ** sounds like "ny" in the word "canyon." Finally, when "q" and "u" are together (**QU**), the pronunciation is "K."

Spanish nouns are masculine or feminine and should be learned with "el" and "la" in front of them. "Los" or "las" is used for plural.

A

airplane	el aeroplano – *ehl ah-eh-roh-'plah-noh*
ambulance	la ambulancia – *lah ahm-boo-'lahn-see-ah*
arm	el brazo – *ehl 'brah-soh*

B

backhoe	la excavadora – *lah ehks-kah-vah-'doh-rah*
bag	la bolsa – *lah 'bohl-sah*
balloon	el balón – *ehl bah-'lohn*
basket	la canasta – *lah kah-'nahs-tah*
beach ball	la pelota de playa – *lah peh-'loh-tah deh 'plah-yah*
bee	la abeja – *lah ah-'beh-hah*
beetle	el escarabajo – *ehl ehs-kah-rah-'bah-hoh*
bench	el banco – *ehl 'bahn-koh*
bicycle	la bicicleta – *lah bee-see-'kleh-tah*
bird	el pájaro – *ehl 'pah-hah-roh*
black	negro – *'neh-groh*
blocks	los cubos – *lohs 'koo-bohs*
blue	azul – *ah-'sool*
book	el libro – *ehl 'lee-broh*
bottle	la botella – *lah boh-'teh-yah*
bottom	el trasero – *ehl trah-'seh-roh*
bread	el pan – *ehl pahn*
brown	marrón – *mahr-'rohn*

brushes, she	ella cepilla – *'eh-yah seh-'pee-yah*
bucket	el balde – *ehl 'bahl-deh*
bus	el autobús – *ehl ow-toh-'boos*
butterfly	la mariposa – *lah mah-ree-'poh-sah*

C

cage	la jaula – *lah 'hah-oo-lah*
cake	la torta – *lah 'tohr-tah*
can	la lata de conservas – *lah 'lah-tah deh kohn-'sehr-vahs*
candy	los caramelos – *lohs kah-rah-'meh-lohs*
car	el automóvil – *ehl ow-toh-'moh-veel*
carries, she	ella lleva – *'eh-yah 'yeh-vah*
caterpillar	la oruga – *lah oh-'roo-gah*
cereal	el cereal – *ehl seh-reh-'ahl*
chair	la silla – *lah 'see-yah*
checkout counter	la caja – *lah 'kah-hah*
cheese	el queso – *ehl 'keh-soh*
chicken	el pollo – *ehl 'poh-yoh*
claps, she	ella aplaude – *'eh-yah ah-'plow-deh*
clock	el reloj – *ehl reh-'loh*
computer	la computadora – *lah kohm-poo-tah-'doh-rah*
cookies	las galletas – *lahs gah-'yeh-tahs*
cow	la vaca – *lah 'vah-kah*
crab	el cangrejo – *ehl kahn-'greh-hoh*
crayons	los gises – *lohs 'hee-sehs*
cries, she	ella llora – *'eh-yah 'yoh-rah*
crocodile	el cocodrilo – *ehl koh-koh-'dree-loh*
cushion	el cojín – *ehl koh-'heen*
cuts, she	ella corta – *'eh-yah 'kohr-tah*

D

dance, they	ellos bailan – *'eh-yohs 'bah-ee-lahn*
day	el día – *ehl 'dee-ah*
dog	el perro – *ehl 'pehr-roh*
doll	la muñeca – *lah moon-'yeh-kah*
dollhouse	la casa de muñecas – *lah 'kah-sah deh moon-'yeh-kahs*
door	la puerta – *lah 'pwehr-tah*
dress	el vestido – *ehl vehs-'tee-doh*
drinks, she	ella bebe – *'eh-yah 'beh-beh*
duck	el pato – *ehl 'pah-toh*
dump truck	el volquete – *ehl vohl-'keh-teh*

E

ears	las orejas – *lahs oh-'reh-hahs*
eats, she	ella come – *'eh-yah 'koh-meh*

eggs	los huevos – *lohs 'hweh-vohs*	jumps, he	él salta – *ehl 'sahl-tah*
eight	ocho – *'oh-choh*	jungle gym	la armazón para trepar – *lah ahr-mah-'sohn 'pah-rah treh-'pahr*
elbow	el codo – *ehl 'koh-doh*		
elephant	el elefante – *ehl eh-leh-'fahn-teh*		
eyes	los ojos – *lohs 'oh-hohs*		

F

face	la cara – *lah 'kah-rah*
farmer	el granjero – *ehl grahn-'heh-roh*
finger	el dedo – *ehl 'deh-doh*
fire engine	la bomba de incendios – *lah 'bohm-bah deh een-'sehn-dee-ohs*
fish	el pescado – *ehl pehs-'kah-doh*
five	cinco – *'seen-koh*
flower	la flor – *lah flohr*
fly	la mosca – *lah 'mohs-kah*
foot	el pie – *ehl pee-'eh*
four	cuatro – *'kwah-troh*
French fries	las papas fritas – *lahs 'pah-pahs 'free-tahs*
Friday	viernes – *vee-'ehr-nehs*
fruit	la fruta – *lah 'froo-tah*
fruit juice	el jugo de fruta – *ehl 'hoo-goh deh 'froo-tah*

G

garage	el garaje – *ehl gah-'rah-heh*
gate	la barrera – *lah bahr-'reh-rah*
giraffe	la jirafa – *lah hee-'rah-fah*
gloves	los guantes – *lohs 'gwahn-tehs*
glue	el pegamento – *ehl peh-gah-'mehn-toh*
goldfish	el pez de colores – *ehl pehs del koh-'loh-rehs*
green	verde – *'vehr-deh*

H

hair	el cabello – *ehl kah-'beh-yoh*
hamburger	la hamburguesa – *lah ahm-boor-'geh-sah*
hamster	el hámster – *ehl 'ahms-tehr*
hand	la mano – *lah 'mah-noh*
hat	el gorro – *ehl 'gohr-roh*
hay	el heno – *ehl 'eh-noh*
head	la cabeza – *lah kah-'beh-sah*
helicopter	el helicóptero – *ehl eh-lee-'kohp-teh-roh*
hen	la gallina – *lah gah-'yee-nah*
horse	el caballo – *ehl kah-'bah-yoh*
hot air balloon	el globo – *ehl 'gloh-boh*
house	la casa – *lah 'kah-sah*

I J

ice cream	el helado – *ehl eh-'lah-doh*
jacket	la chaqueta – *lah chah-'keh-tah*
jar	el tarro – *ehl 'tahr-roh*
jigsaw puzzle	el rompecabezas – *ehl rohm-peh-kah-'beh-sahs*

K

kangaroo	el canguro – *ehl kahn-'goo-roh*
kiddie pool	la piscinita – *lah pees-see-'nee-tah*
kitten	el gatito – *ehl gah-'tee-toh*
knee	la rodilla – *lah roh-'dee-yah*

L

ladybug	la mariquita – *lah mah-ree-'kee-tah*
laughs, he	el ríe – *ehl 'ree-eh*
lawnmower	la cortadora de césped – *lah kohr-tah-'doh-rah deh 'sehs-pehd*
leg	la pierna – *lah pee-'ehr-nah*
lion	el león – *ehl leh-'ohn*

M

mask	la máscara – *lah 'mahs-kah-rah*
milk	la leche – *lah 'leh-cheh*
Monday	lunes – *'loo-nehs*
money	el dinero – *ehl dee-'neh-roh*
motorbike	la moto – *lah 'moh-toh*
mouth	la boca – *lah 'boh-kah*

N

night	la noche – *lah 'noh-cheh*
nightgown	la camisa de dormir – *lah kah-'mee-sah deh dohr-'meer*
nine	nueve – *noo-'eh-veh*
nose	la nariz – *lah nah-'rees*
neck	el cuello – *ehl 'kweh-yoh*

O

one	uno – *'oo-noh*
orange	anaranjado – *ah-nah-rahn-'hah-doh*

P

paints, he	él pinta – *ehl 'peen-tah*
paintbrush	el pincel – *ehl peen-'sehl*
pajamas	el pijama – *ehl pee-'yah-mah*
panda	el panda – *ehl 'pahn-dah*
panties	las bragas – *lahs 'brah-gahs*

pants	los pantalones – *lohs pahn-tah-'loh-nehs*	spaghetti	el espagueti – *ehl ehs-pah-'geh-tee*
parakeet	el periquito – *ehl peh-ree-'kee-toh*	spider	la araña – *lah ah-'rahn-yah*
party hat	el gorro de fiesta – *ehl 'gohr-roh deh fee-'ehs-tah*	street light	el farol – *ehl fah-'rohl*
		stroller	el cochecito de niños – *ehl koh-cheh-'see-toh deh 'neen-yohs*
pink	rosado – *roh-'sah-doh*	sun	el sol – *ehl sohl*
pizza	la pizza – *lah 'pee-tsah*	Sunday	domingo – *doh-'meen-goh*
policeman	el policía – *ehl poh-lee-'see-ah*	sweater	el suéter – *ehl 'sweh-tehr*
present	el regalo – *ehl reh-'gah-loh*	swing	el columpio – *ehl koh-'loom-pee-oh*
puppet	la marioneta – *lah mah-ree-oh-'neh-tah*		
puppy	el perrito – *ehl pehr-'ree-toh*	**T**	
purple	violeta – *vee-oh-'leh-tah*	teacher	la maestra – *lah mah-'ehs-trah*
		teddy bear	el osito de felpa – *ehl oh-'see-toh deh 'fehl-pah*
R			
rabbit	el conejo – *ehl koh-'neh-hoh*	teeth	los dientes – *lohs dee-'ehn-tehs*
rain	la lluvia – *lah 'yoo-vee-ah*	telephone	el teléfono – *ehl teh-'leh-foh-noh*
red	rojo – *'roh-hoh*	television	el televisor – *ehl teh-leh-vee-'sohr*
rice	el arroz – *ehl ahr-'rohs*	ten	diez – *dee-'ehs*
road	el camino – *ehl kah-'mee-noh*	three	tres – *trehs*
rocket	el cohete – *ehl koh-'eh-teh*	thumb	el pulgar – *ehl pool-'gahr*
rollerblades	los patines en línea – *lohs pah-'tee-nehs ehn 'lee-neh-ah*	Thursday	jueves – *hoo-'eh-vehs*
		toe	el dedo del pie – *ehl 'deh-doh dehl pee-'eh*
runs, she	ella corre – *'eh-yah 'kohr-reh*		
		tractor	el tractor – *ehl trahk-'tohr*
S		traffic light	el semáforo – *ehl seh-'mah-foh-roh*
sandcastle	el castillo de arena – *ehl kahs-'tee-yoh del ah-'reh-nah*		
		train	el tren – *ehl trehn*
Saturday	sábado – *'sah-bah-doh*	tree	el árbol – *ehl 'ahr-bohl*
scissors	las tijeras – *lahs tee-'heh-rahs*	truck	el camión – *ehl kah-mee-'ohn*
seagull	la gaviota – *lah gah-vee-'oh-tah*	T-shirt	la camiseta – *lah kah-mee-'seh-tah*
seven	siete – *see-'eh-teh*	Tuesday	martes – *'mahr-tehs*
shell	la concha – *lah 'kohn-chah*	tummy	el vientre – *ehl vee-'ehn-treh*
ship	el barco – *ehl 'bahr-koh*	two	dos – *dohs*
shirt	la camisa – *lah kah-'mee-sah*		
shoes	los zapatos – *lohs sah-'pah-tohs*	**U V W**	
shop	la tienda – *lah tee-'ehn-dah*	vegetables	las legumbres – *lahs leh-'goom-brehs*
shopping cart	la carretilla de compras – *lah kahr-reh-'tee-yah deh 'kohm-prahs*		
		walks, he	él camina – *ehl kah-'mee-nah*
shorts	el pantalón corto – *ehl pahn-tah-'lohn 'kohr-toh*	watering pail	la regadera – *lah reh-gah-'deh-rah*
		wave	la ola – *lah 'oh-lah*
shoulder	el hombro – *ehl 'ohm-broh*	Wednesday	miércoles – *mee-'ehr-koh-lehs*
shovel	la pala – *lah 'pah-lah*	whale	la ballena – *lah bah-'yeh-nah*
sings, he	él canta – *ehl 'kahn-tah*	wheelbarrow	la carretilla – *lah kahr-reh-'tee-yah*
six	seis – *'seh-ees*	wheelchair	la silla de ruedas – *lah 'see-yah deh 'rweh-dahs*
skateboard	el monopatín – *ehl moh-noh-pah-'teen*		
		white	blanco – *'blahn-koh*
skirt	la falda – *lah 'fahl-dah*	wind	el viento – *ehl vee-'ehn-toh*
slide	el tobogán – *ehl toh-boh-'gahn*	window	la ventana – *lah vehn-'tah-nah*
snail	el caracol – *ehl kah-rah-'kohl*	worm	el gusano – *ehl goo-'sah-noh*
snow	la nieve – *lah nee-'eh-veh*		
socks	los calcetines – *lohs kahl-seh-'tee-nehs*	**X Y Z**	
		yellow	amarillo - *ah-mah-'ree-yoh*
sofa	el sofá – *ehl soh-'fah*	yogurt	el yogur - *ehl yoh-'goor*

48